Cocktails in Tahiti

The Best Cocktails
from the World's Most Beautiful Islands

Richard Bondurant

Tahiti Publishing Company

Published: Tahiti Publishing, Inc.,
Atlanta, GA
ISBN-13: 978-1-933850-07-8
ISBN-10: 1-933850-07-8

Book and Cover Design by Bob Swingle of
Lightbourne, Inc.

Disclaimers:
Flowers and other accessories in the drink
photos are for decoration only and are not
edible.

While the publisher and author have used
their best efforts in preparing this book, they
make no representation or warranties with
respect to the accuracy or completeness of the
content of this book and specifically disclaim
any implied warranties of merchantability
or fitness for a particular purpose. Neither
the publisher nor the author can accept
responsibility for any consequences arising
from the use thereof or from information
contained within. The advice and strategies
contained herein may not be suitable for your
situation. You should consult with a professional where appropriate. Neither the publisher nor author shall be liable for any loss of
profit or any other commercial damages
including but not limited to special, incidental,
consequential or other damages.

Printed in Hong Kong

Dedication:

I dedicate this book to John Bettis and Anthony Surratt
and thank them for their assistance in making this book
a reality. Their support, friendship, and knowledge were
a great help to me.

Acknowledgements:

I want to thank Bob Swingle and the staff at Lightbourne,
Inc., for their patience and creativity in working with us
to design an attractive book that captures the beauty of
Tahiti for our readers. I would also like to extend a special thank you to all of the hotels of French Polynesia
who participated in the book.

Contents

An Introduction to Cocktails in Tahiti

The islands of Tahiti captivate our emotions and senses unlike any other place because they are truly the most beautiful and romantic destination on Earth. In fact, mere mention of Tahiti evokes a myriad of tranquil images: turquoise lagoons . . . lush tropical islands . . . majestic mountain peaks . . . warm, caressing breezes . . . romantic evenings . . . dream-like accommodations.

Perhaps you've already vacationed in our beautiful islands and experienced the peaceful ambiance first-hand, or maybe you're planning a trip or have only dreamed of visiting. Whatever the case, you may find yourself yearning to be far from the chaos and maddening pace of your hectic daily life. What you wouldn't give for a taste of life in Tahiti; for the feel of white sand beneath your feet; for a day of sun-drenched meditation by an azure lagoon; for snorkeling in clear, warm waters; for a cool, tropical drink so refreshingly decadent it almost feels like taboo.

Cocktails in Tahiti can't purchase you a plane ticket to Tahiti, but our tropical drinks *will* whisk you to that fantasy of the mind where palm trees sway, gentle waters lap at the shore, and a romantic rendezvous can unfold at any time under a star-filled sky. Whatever your Tahiti fantasy, we can help you conjure it with tasty, tropical libations certain to fill your senses with memories and dreams of our islands.

Delicious, glamorous, even sexy—Tahiti's tropical cocktails are always in style. Whether you want to throw a great party or simply spice up an otherwise normal evening, *Cocktails in Tahiti* provides all of the inspiration and instruction you need. Mixing your own Tahiti cocktails is not only fun but surprisingly easy. We provide an entertaining, practical guide with tools and tips to make you a Tahiti cocktail expert: from how to frost a glass, mix a cocktail, and sculpt a garnish to understanding distinguishing characteristics of various rums and liqueurs.

Our selection of drinks from Earth's paradise ranges from the classics to today's sophisticated drink innovations inspired by some of the world's finest resorts. You'll discover the mysteries behind the famously potent Zombie and Trader Vic Bergeron's legendary and powerful Mai Tai—signature drinks that still retain the rich memories and timeless pleasures from a Tahiti of long ago. Of course, there are modern creations, including the Taha'a Vanilla Martini. This cocktail is crafted from the finest locally grown vanilla and inspired by our vanilla island, Taha'a, whose breezes are often laced with fragrance from the local vanilla plantations. For something equally creative and tasty, you'll find the Bora Bora Nui Resort and Spa's signature cocktail, a tempting treat made with dark rum, a palate of delightful liqueurs, fruit juices, and hints of strawberry jam.

Ultimately, our collection of sun-caressed cocktails captures the spirit of Tahiti without your ever having to leave home. From Tahitian Tea to the Bora Bora Blue Cosmopolitan, these inspired creations can bring you closer to our idyllic shores. Please enjoy our medley of tropical elixirs, and as we say in Tahiti, *Manuia!*

Becoming a Tahiti Cocktail Master

Making your Tahiti drinks will be much easier and the results far more spectacular if you first learn some basic techniques and invest in the appropriate utensils and ingredients. A glass of perfected Tahitian bliss takes only a few basic bar skills, and *Cocktails in Tahiti* includes all of the necessary tips, tools, and instructions to put you on the inside track to becoming an accomplished Tahiti cocktail master.

TOOLS AND EQUIPMENT

You need only a few bar accessories to produce your Tahitian concoctions. You can find them at most liquor stores, retail department stores, and home stores like Williams-Sonoma, Crate & Barrel, and Pottery Barn. In addition, all of these items can be found for sale through the Internet via online retailers.

Bar Spoon: Primarily used for stirring and measuring ingredients, the bar spoon, with its long spiraling handle, can also be used as a crushing device for flavoring ingredients and to assist with the gentle pouring required for layering drinks.

Blender: This is the must-have item for blending fruity cocktails. We recommend a durable model with multiple speeds, but any model that can reduce crushed ice to a smooth consistency will do the job.

Citrus Juicer: This simple tool is invaluable because it saves you from the tedious chore of hand-squeezing juice. Several types are available.

Cocktail Shaker: This is an absolute must and one of the most important pieces of equipment for an aspiring Tahiti cocktail master. A shaker is used to mix drinks with ingredients that are difficult to combine otherwise. There are many styles of shakers, but we prefer the more orthodox stainless steel shaker with the built-in strainer and tightly fitted top. The beauty of this hip, elegant, essential bar tool is the simplicity of its make, shake, and strain quickness.

Cutting Board: A wooden or synthetic cutting board is a necessity for cutting fruit and other items.

Jigger/Measure/Shot Glass: The first thing any aspiring Tahiti cocktail master should acquire is a measure (aka jigger). Guesswork can ruin many delicate cocktails, so careful measuring is important. The classic version is the double-ended steel measure. This small, hourglass-shaped tool will typically have a 1½-ounce measure (a jigger) on one end and a 1-ounce measure (a pony) on the other. An equally useful alternative is the shot glass, with the best ones having gradations indicating ½ ounce to 1½ or 2 ounces.

Ice Bucket: Often the centerpiece of the Tahiti cocktail bar, ice buckets are not only functional but can add an elegant, decorative touch. There are several sophisticated styles available, from silver to crystal.

Measuring Spoons: For measuring fine quantities of ingredients, it's best to have a plastic or metal set with a complete range of spoon sizes up to a full tablespoon.

Measuring Cup: While not as critical as measuring spoons, a measuring cup with markings for ounces will help you with juice and ice measurements.

Mixing Pitcher or Glass: Useful for stirring cocktails served with ice, a tall glass pitcher is perfect for stirring clear Martinis or for mixing more than two drink servings at once. The classic pitcher has a tight, curved lip that holds the ice back when pouring. If you prefer to use a small mixing glass, be certain to use a bar strainer that fits over the top of the glass when pouring.

Muddler: Some cocktails require muddling, crushing, or grinding pieces of fruit, herbs, sugar, or other ingredients in the glass by using a muddler. Most quality bar spoons will have a muddler at the top of the spoon.

Paring Knife: We recommend a paring knife around four inches long and an ordinary, sharp kitchen knife about seven to eight inches long with a spear-like tip useful for more detailed cutting when slicing ingredients such as small fruits or when preparing a garnish.

Stirring Rod: Usually part of a mixing pitcher set, the stirring rod is used to stir cocktails in the mixing pitcher or mixing glass.

Swizzle Stick: Great as a decoration and practical for allowing guests to stir their drinks, swizzle sticks come in a variety of styles: from plastic, kitschy tropical tikis and palm trees to slender, elegantly designed sterling silver versions.

Vegetable Peeler: The vegetable peeler is useful for removing large strips of citrus peel and creating twists for use as garnish.

Zester: Used for producing zest as an ingredient or garnish, a zester is a sharp metal tool with a row of tiny holes on one end.

*Other necessary items include bottle/can openers, cocktail napkins, plastic straws, toothpicks and cocktail spears (for garnishes), and, of course, a set of miniature cocktail umbrellas to decorate your Tahiti drinks!

GLASSWARE

Each recipe in this book includes a recommended style of glassware for serving, and the various styles are summarized here. High-quality, thin-rimmed, elegant glassware boosts any drinking experience and can set a mood for tropical fun and romance. However, you don't need an extensive collection of expensive glasses. A few basic styles are more than sufficient, and virtually every cocktail can be served in a wine glass, if you prefer.

Cocktail Glass/Martini Glass: If a cocktail glass is called for, it refers to the sleek, elegantly stemmed glass with a V-shaped bowl often referred to as a Martini glass and ranging in size from 3 to 8 ounces. It epitomizes the essential elegance of any self-respecting Martini. However, this glass is used for a wide range of straight-up (without ice) cocktails.

Highball Glass: Maybe the most versatile of all bar glasses, the highball glass is best used for drinks containing ice. It's straight-sided and comes in a range of sizes, from 8 to 10 ounces to a taller 10- to 16-ounce glass known as a chimney or Collins glass.

Collins Glass: A taller version of the highball glass, the Collins glass is often used for exotic specialty drinks and holds 10 to 16 ounces, making it ideal for multiple-ingredient drinks and juice cocktails.

Old-Fashioned Glass: Often referred to as a "rocks" glass, this straight-edged, round, stocky 6- to 10-ounce tumbler should have a heavy bottom that will stand up to muddling lemons or limes; it's ideally suited for drinks served over ice.

Hurricane Glass: The hurricane glass is a tall, short-stemmed, elegantly cut glass with a slight curve in the body. Named after its hurricane lamp-like shape, it's the perfect glass for many of our more exotic Tahiti cocktails and comes in sizes ranging from 15 to 22 ounces.

Margarita Glass: This slightly larger and rounded approach to a cocktail glass has a thick, broad rim for holding salt or sugar and is ideal for margaritas. It's also frequently used for daiquiris and other fruit drinks and ranges in size from 12 to 16 ounces.

Champagne Flute: Tall, thin-stemmed, and elegant, this tulip-shaped glass is designed specifically for preserving the effervescence in champagne and comes in sizes ranging from 6 to 8 ounces.

White Wine Glass: Clear and thin-stemmed, the white wine glass features a wide, elongated oval bowl tapering inward at the rim and ranges in size from 10 to 14 ounces.

Red Wine Glass: Also clear and thin-stemmed, the red wine glass features a round bowl tapering inward at the rim and ranges in size from 6 to 10 ounces.

GARNISHES

As you mix your chosen Tahiti cocktail, remember that festive garnishes enhance any drink. Whether you choose understated elegance or over-the-top kitsch, we invite you to accessorize your Tahiti cocktail with a fun, creative, artistic, and romantic flair.

Slices of fresh fruit can be used in numerous ways to create delicious and whimsical touches, while delicate tropical flowers and exotic fruit twists lend a sophisticated and classic design. No matter what components you select, your garnish will dress up your Tahiti cocktail with style.

Kitsch as Garnish

Cocktails in Tahiti are always festive by nature. There's no limit to the number of ways you can adorn your drink, and we encourage you to have fun. If you ever needed an excuse to use those eccentric, outrageous, kitschy cocktail accessories you've been saving, then go

for it! Whether it's the classic paper umbrella, the plastic palm tree swizzle stick, or even a wooden tiki rising from the glass, this is your chance to let loose and jazz up even the most serious drink. Anything goes!

Flowers as Garnish

Flowers commonly found in Tahiti, such as bougainvillea, tiaré, and hibiscus, add an exotic island touch to any of our cocktails. When using a flower, simply rinse it very gently under cool water. You can float the flower or petals directly on the top of the cocktail; you can also skewer them with a cocktail pick alone or in combination with fresh fruit and balance them on the rim of the glass.

Bougainvillea: Bougainvillea flowers add a beautiful and unique touch as garnish. Found in shades of white, red, purple, yellow, and orange, they are abundant across the islands of Tahiti.

Tiaré: The tiaré flower is truly the emblem of Tahiti. Snowy-white in color, the tiaré is shaped like a star with six or eight petals and has a sensuous and intoxicating fragrance reminiscent of the gardenia.

Hibiscus: The wild hibiscus, called *hau* by Tahitians, grows abundantly in Tahiti. Hibiscus flowers have been bred to include many beautiful colors; they make excellent decorations for any Tahiti cocktail.

Fruits as Garnish or Juice

From bananas and mangos to coconuts and lemons, we'll cover all the essentials to prepare you for slicing, squeezing, and cutting the fruits used to craft the perfect Tahiti cocktail.

All of the recipes in this book call for fruits that are readily available in one form or another. Naturally, using fresh, ripe fruit or freshly squeezed juice will always give you the best flavor. But when you can't find fresh, you can purchase frozen whole and cut fruits and juices from most grocery stores. Working with some fresh fruits can present a challenge, and in those instances, frozen juices or precut fruits can offer a practical alternative.

Fruit wedges such as oranges, pineapples, limes, or lemons are fast and easy to create. First, wash and dry the fruit. Remove both ends and slice it in half around the center or from top to bottom. Next, cut each half into four equal wedges. Make a small slit in the middle of each wedge so you can place the garnish on, not in, the glass. Wedges not only look nice; they're functional, too. By squeezing the wedges, guests can easily add extra flavor to their cocktail.

Twists usually are prepared from grapefruits, lemons, limes, or oranges. To create a twist, start by removing the stem end from the fruit to create a flat base that will allow it to "stand." Stand the fruit upright on a cutting board and use a paring knife, working from top to bottom, to cut $1/2$-inch-wide strips of rind that incorporate a small amount of the inner white pith. To add the twist to a cocktail, hold the twist, colored-side down, about an inch above the top of the drink. Gently squeeze the twist to release the aromatic oils into the drink. After squeezing, you can rub the colored side of the twist around the rim of the glass to add additional flavor. The twist can be placed in the drink or along the rim of the glass as decoration.

Wheels or slices of fruits like lemons, oranges, limes, pineapples, and grapefruits are prepared by first removing both ends from the fruit; cut deep enough to expose the pulp. For wheels, cut the fruit into thin slices with the rind intact for color and visual texture. Wheels can be used whole or cut in half. To place the wheel on the glass, cut through the peel and halfway into the pulp to create a slit that will allow you to "hang" the fruit over the lip of the glass. You can also leave the slice uncut and place it as a floating garnish in the drink.

Spirals can be created by using a vegetable peeler or canella knife to remove a single long, narrow strip of a fruit's peel. Begin at one end of the fruit, and work your way around it slowly paring off the peel in a continuous strip. Twist the pared peel around your finger to intensify the spiral effect. Slowly drop the spiral into the drink or hang it on the edge of the glass.

Flags are prepared by spearing a maraschino cherry with other fruits onto a cocktail skewer or toothpick. A cherry speared onto an orange slice is called an orange flag; speared onto a pineapple, it's called a pineapple flag, and so on.

Zest (the colored portion of a fruit's shiny outer peel) is created by using a fine-holed grater or a zest remover.

Lemons, limes, oranges, and grapefruits are most commonly used to create zest. You can use it to coat glass rims or sprinkle it directly on top of a drink.

Bananas: In Tahiti, most bananas are harvested when they're bright green because they develop a better taste when ripened off the tree. To prepare, simply peel back the skin of the banana. After peeling it, you can slice it crosswise for use in blended drinks or as a garnish. You should always prepare bananas as close as possible to serving time because, once peeled, the flesh of a banana can discolor quickly. Slices can be placed as wheels on the rim of a drink or speared with other fruit on a cocktail pick as decoration.

Coconuts: The coconut tree is often called the "life tree" by Tahitians because of its historic importance in their lives. Large coconut plantations still cover many islands, and numerous qualities of the coconut lend themselves to creating many of our Tahiti cocktails.

- *Coconut Milk: The white liquid extracted by pressing and squeezing the coconut meat*
- *Coconut Water: The clear liquid drained from a coconut by piercing its "eyes"*
- *Coconut Cream: A thick, rich cream skimmed from coconut milk*

Coconut meat can be used in several ways to garnish a Tahiti cocktail. While using fresh coconut will always give you the best flavor, opening a coconut can be quite tedious. As a result, you may prefer to simply purchase shredded dried coconut, coconut cream, coconut milk, or coconut water, all of which are available in grocery stores. If, however, you plan to use a fresh coconut, look

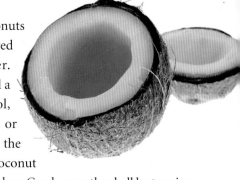

for "easy crack" coconuts that have been scored around the center. Using a hammer and a sharp, pointed tool, such as an ice pick or screw driver, pierce the eyes and drain the coconut water into a bowl or glass. Crack open the shell by tapping it with the hammer around the scored center line. If the coconut hasn't been prescored around the center, wrap it in a towel and hit it a few times with the hammer to open it. Cut out the white meat and remove any of the brown skin from the meat. For a garnish, you can grate the meat with a grater or use a paring knife to pare off paper-thin slices to sprinkle on top of your cocktail. You can also use a wedge of the coconut meat in combination with other fruits on a cocktail skewer or cut a slit in a small slice of coconut and balance it on the rim of the glass.

Grapefruits: As a garnish, grapefruits are most often used as zest, wheels, twists, and spirals. First introduced to Tahiti in the early 20th century, the grapefruit is now one of the most common fruits found throughout the islands. However, because of the grapefruit's acidity, Tahitians typically prefer the sweeter tastes of oranges and pineapples; in fact, the largest grapefruit plantation in Tahiti has been converted to a golf course.

Kiwifruit Slices: This unusual fruit has a brown, fuzzy skin and radiant green flesh speckled with hundreds of tiny, edible black seeds. With a sweet flavor and tart finish, it makes a wonderful garnish when sliced into wheels and balanced on the rim of a cocktail glass.

Lemons: As a garnish, lemons are extremely colorful and versatile and can be used as zest, twists, wheels, wedges, and spirals for a fun addition to any drink. Lemon rinds have wonderful aromatic oils that can add an acidic kick to your cocktail when twisted or dropped into the drink.

Limes: Limes are just as versatile as lemons, with similar aromatic oils that can be released by twisting and dropping the rind into the drink.

Mangos: This sweet and fragrant fruit was introduced to Tahiti in 1848. It was quickly adopted by the Tahitian people, who used its trunk to build canoes. Ripe mangos make a beautiful garnish because of their bright orange flesh and intoxicating flavors. To prepare a mango, use a sharp knife to pare off the skin. Place the mango on its side and slice off the meat lengthwise as close as you can to the flat seed at the center. You can place a whole mango slice vertically into a drink or create a small slit in the slice and balance it on the rim of the glass.

Maraschino Cherries: Many people enjoy eating this colorful and tasty garnish, so always use maraschino cherries with stems attached to provide a helpful way of removing the cherry from the cocktail. The red maraschino cherry is sweet; the less common green maraschino cherry has a strong, minty flavor.

Melons: Melon garnishes, such as watermelon, honeydew, or cantaloupe, add an unusual textural artistry to a cocktail. Two varieties are cultivated in Tahiti, predominantly on the motus surrounding the islands of Maupiti and Huahine. The first variety is a small, deep-green, rounded fruit, and the other is a larger, more elongated fruit with a pale-green skin. The watermelon and honeydew can be cut into wedges or slices and hung on the rim of the glass. Melon balls, which can be created using a melon scoop, make a colorful cocktail decoration when speared onto a cocktail skewer or toothpick and balanced on the rim of the glass.

Olives (green): The classic garnish for a Martini, green olives should be served without pimentos, skewered on a toothpick or cocktail skewer, and placed directly into the drink.

Oranges: Oranges are a great garnish for a Tahiti cocktail and can be used as zest, twists, wheels, wedges, or spirals. The first orange trees were introduced to Tahiti by early navigators. Tahitians loved the oranges and quickly planted orange trees throughout the islands. Unfortunately, insects and disease wiped out most of the orange trees in the 20th century. Today, only a few wild orange trees survive in Tahiti on isolated mountainous plateaus where they're still harvested each June.

Papayas: Papayas are a staple of the Tahitian diet and are used raw or cooked in many dishes. Papayas have an unusual flavor that is a refreshing mix of sweet and tart. Sliced papaya can be placed directly into a drink or along the edge for a delicious, decorative touch, and diced papaya is a tasty addition to any blended tropical drink. Filled with black seeds, however, papayas can be messy to prepare since the seeds should be removed before serving.

Pineapples: For Tahiti cocktail garnishes, the pineapple is the perfect fruit because it can be used from top to bottom. You can even incorporate the spiny leaves as a green accent with other colorful fruit garnishes. The pineapple was introduced to Tahiti by the famous Captain Bligh, who commanded the equally famous ship Bounty. Today, the pineapple is the most cultivated plant in Tahiti. A juice factory has been built on the island of Moorea to process the island's vast production. The pineapple variety found in the islands of Tahiti is very thorny, but its taste is deliciously strong and its yellow flesh wonderfully sweet and fragrant.

Prepare a pineapple by laying it on its side and cutting off the ends. Then cut it crosswise into ⅓-inch-thick slices to create wheels with the rind intact for added color and texture. These wheels can be cut into four or six slices with slits so that they can be placed on the rim of the glass, or they can be quartered to create wedges.

Pineapple shells: For the ultimate fun, playful, tropical garnish, you can serve your Tahiti cocktail in a pineapple shell instead of a glass. Simply cut off the spiny top of a pineapple and, using a sharp knife and spoon, scoop out the flesh, leaving the shell intact. Refrigerate until ready to use. Save the fruit and juice for making drinks.

Vanilla: Tahitian vanilla is a prized treat, and many of our cocktail recipes suggest the use of this delicate ingredient. Known worldwide as perhaps the finest of vanillas, the *vanilla tahitiensis,* or "Polynesian black gold," is grown almost entirely on the lush, green, remote island of Taha'a—the sweet scent rising through the hillsides. Tahitian vanilla is a type of orchid, and unlike more common varieties that are pollinated naturally by birds or bees, each Tahitian vanilla flower must be lovingly pollinated by hand at just the right moment. Dried

Tahitian vanilla beans can be placed whole into a cocktail or crushed and sprinkled on the surface.

MIXING TECHNIQUES

Before pouring your Tahiti cocktail, you should be aware of a few hints to enhance your mixology skills. There are five basic ways to create a cocktail: shaking, stirring, building, blending, and layering. Whichever method you use, accurately measure the ingredients first to achieve that all-important balance of tastes.

Always put ice in the mixing container first so the ice will chill the ingredients as they're added; this also lessens dilution of the liquor.

Shaking Drinks: Using a shaker is the most enjoyable way to mix a cocktail. As a general rule, drinks made with fruit juices, milk, cream, and liqueurs should be shaken before served. Use a cocktail shaker with a lid and built-in strainer. Shaking can dilute a drink by up to 25% and mixes the ingredients very well, producing a nice foamy head when the mixture contains juices. The object of shaking is to nearly freeze the drink while breaking down and combining the ingredients.

To shake a drink in a standard shaker, fill the container with ice according to the recipe, add the ingredients, put the cap in place, and then top with the lid. Grasp with both hands, one hand on top and one supporting the base, and give a short, sharp, snappy shake. You should always shake a drink vigorously for a relatively short time (about 10 seconds) to chill it sufficiently without diluting it too much. Shake too little and you'll get an unchilled, unblended cocktail; too much and you'll end up with a cold but watery one. Take the lid off and strain the drink into the glass using the built-in strainer in the cocktail shaker cap. If the drink is to be served over ice, strain it into a glass full of fresh ice cubes; never pour the drink, partially melted cubes and all, directly from the shaker into an empty glass. If you're serving the drink straight-up (without ice), strain the cocktail into a chilled glass.

Stirring Drinks: Stirring a drink is the best method for retaining clarity and strength of spirits. You can stir cocktails effectively with a metal or glass rod in a mixing glass or mixing pitcher. When using a mixing pitcher or mixing glass, use ice cubes instead of crushed ice to prevent dilution. Stir the contents until the pitcher or mixing glass begins to collect condensation. Strain the cocktail into the serving glass. You can stir drinks in a special mixing pitcher (sometimes called a martini pitcher) with a spout that catches ice and negates the need for a strainer.

Building Drinks: When building a cocktail, simply pour the measured ingredients directly into an ice-filled glass. Usually, the ingredients are stirred together in the glass using a swizzle stick or straw that remains in the drink when served.

Blending Drinks: This method involves pouring the ingredients into a blender, usually with crushed ice, and flipping the switch. Blending is used for recipes containing fruit or other ingredients that don't break down by shaking, and it's an appropriate way of combining these ingredients with others to create a smooth, ready-to-serve mixture. A perfect consistency is reached when a straw can stand up in the middle of the blended drink. Blending dilutes drinks by up to 40%, so blended drinks require very strongly flavored ingredients. The key to a great blended drink is knowing how much ice and liquid to include. It's better to underestimate the liquid ingredients because you can always add more liquid if necessary; too much liquid, however, will ruin a blended drink.

Layering and Floating Drinks: This technique is used to add multiple layers of color or texture to drinks. When making a layered drink, the liqueur or liquor with the highest density should be poured into the glass first, followed by the one with the next-highest density, and so forth. Thus, the ingredients will form layers floating one atop the other. After pouring the first liquor into the glass, pour each successive liquor over the back of a bar spoon so it drizzles gently, rather than pours, onto the preceding liquor. Rest the rounded part of the spoon against the inside of the glass and slowly pour the ingredient down the back of the spoon. The ingredient should run down the inside of the glass and remain separated from the ingredient below it.

ADDITIONAL TIPS FOR MAKING THE PERFECT TAHITI COCKTAIL

Bar Ingredients

From spirits to juice, a drink is only as good as its ingredients. You can't make cheap rum taste like premium rum, so buy the best ingredients (including mixers) your budget will allow. For example, a daiquiri made with first-rate rum deserves fresh lime juice and fresh fruit to retain the high quality.

You'll find that just a few key ingredients are used in producing our selection of tasty tropical libations, so stock your bar with the following: maraschino cherries, granulated sugar, Tahitian vanilla extract, margarita salt, real grenadine (made from pomegranates), lime juice, pineapple juice, cranberry juice, lemon juice, and simple syrup.

Simple Syrup

A commonly used bar ingredient worth making and keeping on hand, simple syrup is also referred to as sugar syrup. It's often used to balance the tart citrus flavors of many tropical libations. Making simple syrup is quick and easy, and it will keep for many months.

Simple Syrup Recipe: Makes 2¾ cups
2 cups granulated sugar
2 cups water

In a small saucepan, combine the sugar and water. Cook three to six minutes over medium heat, stirring frequently, until the sugar completely dissolves and the syrup is clear. Do not boil. Remove the pan from the heat and allow the syrup to cool. Pour the simple syrup into a bottle or jar; we suggest a bottle fitted with a professional pouring spout for easy serving.

Chilling a Glass

Unless otherwise specified, always chill a glass before serving a cocktail in it. Prechilled glasses from the freezer are the best way to keep your drinks cold, and most cocktails taste better cold. You can chill a glass several ways: by refrigerating it for an hour, placing it in the freezer for 20 minutes, or burying it in a pan of cracked or shaved ice. If you need a chilled glass pronto, fill the glass with cracked ice and cold water and chill it while you're mixing drinks. Toss out the ice, wipe off any excess water, and pour in the drink. When using fine crystal, chill it in the refrigerator or use the cracked ice chilling method to avoid cracking the glass. Chilling is especially important for drinks served in goblet, hurricane, Martini, or Collins glasses.

Frosting a Glass

Rinsing a glass in cold water and chilling it in the freezer for 30 to 45 minutes will give it a lovely frosty patina. To frost only the rim of the glass, dip the rim in water and place the glass in the freezer for 30 to 45 minutes.

Ice

Ice is the foundation of good mixing. Never skimp on ice, and make sure it's fresh, clean, free of odors, and frozen hard to the core. Using ice that's at the melting point will dilute your drink quickly, and a watery cocktail is just as unappealing as a warm one. Always put the ice in the mixing container first and the liquor and juices last. This will chill the rest of the ingredients as they're added and lessen the chance of diluting the liquor.

Rimming Glasses

To add elegance and flavor, as well as color and textural appeal, rim your cocktail glasses with sugar (granulated or powdered), sea salt or margarita salt, citrus zest, coconut flakes, or freshly grated coconut. You can also combine rimming ingredients (e.g., citrus zest with salt or sugar, or with grated coconut) to create unique, multidimensional flavor combinations. If you're entertaining a crowd, glasses can be rimmed hours ahead of time; just set the glasses aside, out of harm's way.

For the best results, start with a chilled glass whenever possible, although an unchilled glass can be used when necessary. Begin by placing several tablespoons of the rimming ingredient on a small plate or in a wide-bottom bowl; six to eight tablespoons of the ingredient will rim about four glasses. Shake gently to distribute the ingredient evenly on the plate or in the bowl. Next, rub a lemon, lime, or orange wedge around the rim of the

glass to lightly wet it. Turn the glass upside down, gently place the rim directly into the ingredient, and carefully turn the glass back and forth to coat the rim completely. Pull the rim gently out of the ingredient and tap or shake the glass lightly to remove any excess ingredient. When adding ice or pouring your cocktail into the glass, be careful not to disturb the coated rim.

Muddling

Muddling is used to extract the most flavor from certain fresh ingredients such as fruit or mint garnishes. Crush the ingredient directly inside your cocktail glass using a pestle or the muddler on the back side of your bar spoon.

Fresh Juice

It probably goes without saying, but whenever possible, use the freshest ingredients—especially fresh-squeezed juices. There's a tremendous flavor difference between fresh-squeezed and bottled or frozen juices.

Grenadine

Pomegranate juice is the basis for true grenadine syrup. Some products on the market are labeled as grenadine but are actually nothing more than colored corn syrup. Buy only real grenadine made from pomegranates.

MEASURING

Always measure your ingredients carefully, and don't guess—especially when serving guests. The easiest way to ruin a great drink is to NOT use the proper amount of spirits or mixers; even a dash too much or too little of one ingredient can unbalance the delicate mix of flavors. On the other hand, that doesn't mean you can't experiment on your own—just think, you may create a concoction you like better than the original recipe! There are four simple ingredients in many Tahiti drinks: lime juice, simple syrup, pineapple juice, and rum. Adding or adjusting the amounts of these items is the easiest way to explore new Tahiti cocktail tastes, if you want to experiment.

To assist you with measuring, here are some helpful conversion tables.

Conversion Table

1/4 ounce = 2 teaspoons
1/2 ounce = 1 tablespoon
3/4 ounce = 1/2 jigger,
or 1 tablespoon + 2 teaspoons
1 ounce = 2 tablespoons
1 1/2 ounces = 1 jigger
3 ounces = 2 jiggers
8 ounces = 1 cup
32 ounces = 1 quart
1 teaspoon = 1/8 ounce
1 tablespoon = 1/2 ounce
Bar spoon = 1/2 ounce
1/4 cup = 2 ounces
1/3 cup = 2 1/2 ounces
1/2 cup = 4 ounces
2/3 cup = 5 ounces
3/4 cup = 6 ounces
1 cup = 8 ounces
1 pint = 16 ounces
1 quart = 32 ounces

1 liter	= 33.8 ounces
1 fifth	= 25½ ounces
1 jigger	= 1½ ounces or 3 tablespoons
1 pony	= 1 ounce
Dash	= 2 to 3 drops
Scoop of ice	= 1 cup
Scoop of ice cream	= ½ cup
1 medium lemon	= 3 tablespoons juice
1 medium lime	= 2 tablespoons juice
1 medium orange	= ⅓ cup juice

U.S. to Metric

1 teaspoon	= 5 milliliters
1 tablespoon	= 15 milliliters
1 fluid ounce	= 30 milliliters
⅓ cup	= 80 milliliters
1 cup	= 240 milliliters
2 cups (1 pint)	= 470 milliliters
4 cups (1 quart)	= 0.95 liter
4 quarts (1 gallon)	= 3.8 liters

Metric to U.S.

5 milliliters	= 1 teaspoon
15 milliliters	= 1 tablespoon
100 milliliters	= 3.4 fluid ounces
240 milliliters	= 1 cup
1 liter	= 34 fluid ounces
1 liter	= 4.2 cups
1 liter	= 2.1 pints
1 liter	= 1.06 quarts
1 liter	= 0.26 gallon

LIQUORS AND LIQUEURS USED IN TAHITI COCKTAILS

Rum, vodka, gin, and tequila are the main liquors in our cocktail recipes. Knowing the basics of these liquors will help you understand their uses and differences when crafting a delicious Tahiti cocktail. Our recipes specify well-known brand names like Bacardi, Ketel One, Jose Cuervo, Cruzan, Skyy, etc. However, these specific brands are merely a suggestion, and you should feel free to substitute another brand of similar liquor and flavor, if you wish.

Rum

The deep, sweet flavor of rum has a mysterious and enchanting quality that is almost universally associated with tropical drinks. Rum is—literally and figuratively—the central spirit of the Tahiti cocktail and the quintessential ingredient for the true Tahiti flavor experience. In many of our drinks, two or more types of rum will be used to create multidimensional, complex flavors that a single rum can't achieve by itself.

Rum is a product of equatorial countries and, thus, a natural basis for many tropical drinks. The process of making rum involves pressing sugarcane to extract the juice, which is then boiled down to a thick syrup, or molasses, from which the rum is distilled. Rum is then aged from a few months to 10 years.

Light or White Rums: Also called silver or blanco rums, these rums are light-bodied and faintly sweet and are aged less than one year in uncharred white oak barrels or steel tanks. They range in color from clear to pale gold

and are usually filtered through charcoal for smoothness. This aging and filtering process creates the clean, light flavor and aromas of light rums, making them the perfect base ingredient for many Tahiti cocktails. Remember, however, they're delicate and their flavor can be overpowered in cocktails with juices and other strong tastes.

Gold Rums: Medium-bodied rums are often called gold or amber rums and are rich and smooth in flavor. Their color is achieved through a one-to-three-year aging process in charred barrels, and occasionally the color is adjusted with additional caramel coloring. To add a slightly more intense flavor, they may be substituted in cocktails that call for light rum.

Dark Rums: Heavy-bodied, or dark rums are typically used in rum punches and are frequently combined with light rums in many cocktails. Dark rums are aged from three to 12 years in charred oak barrels. Dark, heavy rums add strong and richly sweet flavors to drinks and are best used to gently enhance the lighter rums of our cocktails.

Demerara Rum: Demerara rum, a dark overproof rum, is the secret ingredient in many truly memorable tropical drinks. This prized dark rum is made by distillers in the Demerara region of Guyana. It usually contains a higher proof than other rums and is known for a rich, woody, almost burnt, fragrant flavor. Demerara rum is often used for topping or mixing in Tahiti cocktails, but it can also be sipped straight over ice.

Aged Rums: These are expensive, vintage rums distilled in small batches. They're good for sipping with a splash of tonic and lime—but don't use these rums in a cocktail.

Spiced and Flavored Rums: In the late 20th century, it became popular to flavor rums by using spices and aromatics during the distillation process. Today, the variety of flavored rums exceeds the number of flavored gin and vodka options. Vanilla, citrus, pineapple, coconut, and other fruits and spices are infused in today's flavored and spiced rums. Popular brands of coconut-flavored rums include Cruzan, Parrot Bay, and Malibu, while Captain Morgan is one of the best-known spiced rums. These rums are the basis for many of our Tahiti cocktail recipes.

Overproof Rums: Rums like Bacardi 151 or Demerara are overproof rums. They have a strong taste and higher alcohol content and are used in small amounts. They're often floated on top of a drink and sometimes ignited to create a flaming cocktail. Dark rum can be substituted when a recipe calls for overproof rum.

Vodka

A clear spirit, vodka is believed to have been introduced in the 14th century.

Vodka is one of the easiest spirits to make. Although potatoes and beets are popular alternatives, top brands of vodka are made by fermenting and distilling grains such as barley, wheat, or rye. After being distilled, vodka is filtered using either charcoal or quartz crystals. Distilled water is then added to reduce the vodka to bottle strength. Vodka requires no aging and is ready to drink immediately.

Vodka has no distinct taste. The stylistic variations come from the distinctive textures that different brands of vodka present on the tongue and the way the vodka "feels" in the mouth. Two brands that represent the two prominent styles are Absolut and Stolichnaya. Absolut has an oily, silky-sweet texture, while Stolichnaya is clean and watery with an almost medicinal finish in the mouth. Cheaper brands tend to burn in the mouth and throat, while premium brands are smooth and excellent for shots and Martinis.

Because it has no distinct color, taste, or aroma, vodka is the best mixing liquor. As a category, vodka has been growing at an incredible rate, driven by a surge in the popularity of vodka Martinis and coupled with vodka manufacturers offering numerous flavor choices. Many vodkas are infused with fruit or spice flavorings to create popular flavored versions like lemon, vanilla, and orange that are great for Tahiti cocktails.

Tequila

Tequila, like vodka and rum, has been revolutionized in its forms and popularity during the last several years. Tequila is in vogue and has quickly become the new spirit enjoyed by today's trendy and sophisticated epicureans.

Tequila is made from the blue agave plant and produced primarily in Mexico. The finest tequilas are made with sugar from the blue agave and not a blend of sugars. These high-end tequilas will state "100 percent blue agave" on their labels, indicating that they possess superior taste and were bottled in Mexico.

Silver or White Tequilas: These clear tequilas are freshly distilled and bottled within 60 days. Their taste is harsher and more unrestrained than aged tequilas. However, their stronger flavor makes them perfect for tropical cocktails since the flavor of the tequila is not completely lost in the drink.

Gold Tequilas: Often confused as being aged tequilas, these tequilas are gold merely because caramel coloring and flavoring have been added to silver tequilas, resulting in a slightly gentler flavor. Gold tequilas are popular as shots or in shooters.

Reposado Tequilas: These tequilas are mellowed and improved by aging from two months to a year in oak barrels. Their color comes from the oak barrels and ranges from pale gold to deep gold. Hints of honey and vanilla in these tequilas add a rich, warm dimension to our Tahiti margaritas.

Anejo Tequilas: Anejo means "aged," and these premium tequilas are aged in wood barrels from one to five years. Aged tequilas are highly sought after by connoisseurs and are often sipped on the rocks or straight up. Because of their high price, we don't recommend using Anejo tequilas in our cocktail recipes.

Gin

Gin is a clear spirit created from barley and rye, to which a combination of flavorings derived from special herbs and spices are added. These flavorings, known as botanicals, include aniseed, coriander, fruit peels, and juniper berry. The name gin comes from the French word *genièvre*, meaning "juniper." Unlike other spirits, gin doesn't have a qualification measure by age. Generally speaking, there are two types of gins: London Dry and Genever.

London Dry gin is normally used in preparing a cocktail. Its most obvious use in this book is in our tropical Martinis. However, it works very well in many of our other elegant cocktail recipes. Genever gin is made in the Netherlands and has a very strong, rich, full-bodied, malty flavor that can overwhelm anything it's mixed with; therefore, Genever gin is seldom used in cocktails and is usually enjoyed straight up or over ice.

LIQUEURS AND OTHER SPIRITS

The liqueur category, also known as cordials, is quite extensive. Liqueurs come in virtually every imaginable flavor, color, and alcohol content and are a key flavorful and colorful enhancement to many cocktails in Tahiti.

Liqueurs are sweet and by definition must contain at least 2.5% sugar by weight. However, most are considerably higher in sugar content, and many contain up to 35% of a sweetening agent. If sweetening accounts for less than 10% by weight of the finished product, the liqueur may be labeled dry. Those liqueurs with a very high sugar content have a cream-like thickness and are referred to as crèmes.

Many liqueurs are generic in nature, meaning they're produced and marketed under the same liqueur name by numerous suppliers. Some common varieties include amaretto, grenadine, triple sec, and schnapps. Even among these generic liqueurs, however, there are prominent brand names such as Bols, DeKuyper, and Potters.

There are also many well-known proprietary liqueurs produced from a closely guarded formula and sold under a trademarked name by only one producer. Famous proprietary liqueurs include Bailey's, Chambord, Cointreau, Frangelico, Midori, and Grand Marnier.

A few important notes about some of the liqueurs used in our Tahiti cocktails:

- There's no difference between curaçao and blue curaçao except the color. Both are made from dried orange peels, port wine, and spices.

- Brown and white crème de cacao are also identical except for their color and consist of a blend of vanilla and cocoa beans.

- Grand Marnier is an orange cognac; Cointreau, an orange brandy; Triple Sec, an orange-based liqueur. Each has different uses in mixed drinks and should not be used in place of one another.

LIQUEURS AND OTHER SPIRITS REFERENCE

Alize: Passion fruit-flavored liqueur from France

Amaretto: Italian almond-flavored liqueur

Bailey's: Irish cream liqueur

Banana Liqueur: Banana-flavored liqueur

Chambord: French black raspberry liqueur with herbs and honey

Cointreau: Colorless French brandy-based liqueur flavored from sweet and bitter orange peel

Coconut Liqueur: Coconut-flavored liqueur

Crème d'almond: American version of Crème de Noyeaux

Crème de banana: A sweet, yellow, brandy-based liqueur flavored with bananas

Crème de cacao: Brown or colorless liqueur with a chocolate flavor made from cacao beans and vanilla

Crème de coconut: Coconut-flavored liqueur

Crème de menthe: Mint-flavored liqueur that comes in green, red, and colorless varieties

Crème de Noyeaux: Almond-flavored liqueur produced in France and available in pink or white

Curaçao: Generic term for orange-flavored liqueurs made from the dried peel of a bitter variety of orange and available in white (colorless) and blue varieties

Frangelico: A liqueur made with hazelnuts, berries, and flowers

Grand Marnier: French cognac liqueur with orange flavor; brown in color

Grenadine: Non-alcoholic syrup flavored with pomegranates

Kahlua: Coffee-flavored liqueur from Mexico

Mango liqueur: Mango-flavored liqueur

Midori: Green honeydew melon spirit from Japan

Napolean Mandarine: Belgian orange liqueur made from cognac

Orgeat: Sweet, almond-flavored nonalcoholic syrup

Parfait Amour: Violet-colored liqueur with hints of vanilla and rose petals

Peach Schnapps: Peach-flavored liqueur

Pear Liqueur: Pear-flavored liqueur

Raspberry Liqueur: Raspberry-flavored liqueur (framboise liqueur)

Cocktails in Tahiti

Tahiti Bikini

Ingredients:

- ½ ounce Mt. Gay Eclipse gold rum
- ½ ounce Malibu coconut rum
- ½ ounce Midori melon liqueur
- ½ ounce blue curaçao
- 1½ ounces orange juice
- 1½ ounces pineapple juice

Mixing Instructions:

Combine all ingredients in a cocktail shaker half-filled with ice. Shake well until blended and chilled. Strain into a Collins glass half-filled with ice cubes. Garnish as desired.

The Islands of Tahiti

Tahiti is actually the largest and most populous island of the nation of French Polynesia. Its name, however, is often used to refer collectively to all 118 islands of the nation. Tahiti and her islands cover 2 million square miles of the South Pacific ocean, and the country is composed of five great archipelagos—the Society Islands, Tuamotu Islands, Marquesas Islands, Gambier Islands, and Austral Islands. The Society Islands—Tahiti, Moorea, Bora Bora, Raiatea, and Huahine—are the most visited islands and account for the vast majority of the nation's commerce and population.

The official languages of French Polynesia are French and Tahitian. The Tahitian language was purely oral and non-written until the early 19th century. Tahitian uses only 16 letters: A, B, E, F, G, H, I, K, M, N, O, P, R, T, U, and V. In Tahitian, each letter has a certain sound, and that sound always remains the same regardless of the letter combinations. There are no confusing rules about pronunciation, making Tahitian relatively easy to pronounce. Although it officially exists now, the sound of the letter B was never present in the ancient Tahitian oral language. When European explorers first heard the natives speak of the island of *Pora Pora*, they mistook the pronunciation as *Bora Bora*, and still today, the name Bora Bora continues to be used instead of Pora Pora.

Tahitian Sunrise

Ingredients:
- 1 ounce Jose Cuervo tequila
- ½ ounce Alize passion fruit liqueur
- ½ ounce mango liqueur
- ½ ounce fresh orange juice
- ½ ounce fresh lime juice
- 1 teaspoon powdered sugar
- sugar (granulated)

Mixing Instructions:
Rim a Martini glass with granulated sugar. Combine the remaining ingredients in a cocktail shaker half-filled with ice. Shake well until blended and chilled. Strain into the glass. Garnish as desired.

Pineapple Horn Blower

The population of French Polynesia is approximately 225,000, with nearly 175,000 people living on the main island of Tahiti. The next most populous islands are Raiatea, Moorea, and Bora Bora. Tahiti has a very young population, with over half of its residents falling under the age of 20. Chinese descendants account for 10% of the nation's population and historically have owned most of the nation's retail trade businesses; that's why, when Tahitians talk about going shopping, they often say they're going to "le chinois," meaning "to the Chinese."

Ingredients:

- 1 1/2 ounces Bombay Sapphire gin
- 1 1/2 ounces pineapple juice
- 1/2 ounce lemon juice
- 1/2 ounce simple syrup
- 1 teaspoon Bailey's Irish Cream

Mixing Instructions:

Combine all ingredients in a cocktail shaker half-filled with ice. Shake well until blended and chilled. Strain into a Martini glass. Garnish as desired.

High Islands

Tahitian Tea

The islands of Tahiti, Bora Bora, Moorea, and Huahine are referred to as "high islands" because they have dramatic mountain peaks and tend to be quite lush with many trees and plants. These high islands were formed millions of years ago by underwater volcanoes, and each of them has a coral reef, which surrounds and protects the island from the full force of the sea. Between the reefs and the land are calm, brightly colored lagoons that continually dazzle visitors and photographers with their magnificent beauty.

Ingredients:

- ½ ounce Skyy vodka
- ½ ounce Bacardi light rum
- ½ ounce Beefeater gin
- ½ ounce triple sec
- 3 ounces orange juice
- 3 ounces cranberry juice

Mixing Instructions:

Combine all ingredients in a cocktail shaker half-filled with ice. Shake well until blended and chilled. Strain into a Collins glass half-filled with ice cubes. Garnish with a lime wedge and cherry.

Bora Bora Margarita

Ingredients:

- 1¼ ounces Jose Cuervo Especial gold tequila
- ¾ ounce blue curaçao
- ½ ounce Cointreau
- 1 ounce fresh lime juice
- margarita or sea salt

Mixing Instructions:

Rim a chilled Collins glass with salt and fill with ice. Pour the remaining ingredients into a cocktail shaker half-filled with ice. Shake well until blended and chilled. Strain into the glass. Garnish as desired.

Majestic Mounts

That Tahitian word for Bora Bora is actually *Pora Pora* and means "first born." As legend has it, Bora Bora was the first island to emerge from the waters after the creation of Raiatea. Dominating Bora Bora are majestic Mount Otemanu and Mount Pahia, two towering volcanic peaks of black rock that jut out of the center of the emerald-green island. Their summits are often draped in white clouds, which cause these landmarks to take on mysterious and mythical qualities. With these two stunning peaks and its brilliant turquoise lagoon, Bora Bora offers the most dramatic beauty of any island in French Polynesia.

Raiatea, Birthplace of Gods

Raiatea Island Soda

Raiatea, the second-largest island in French Polynesia, is located 120 miles northwest of the island of Tahiti. Ancient Tahitians believed Raiatea to be the sacred birthplace of their gods, as well as the home of their religious and cultural beginnings. The most important and well-preserved religious site in all of Polynesia is located on Raiatea. It is from Raiatea that the first Polynesian tribes set out to colonize Hawaii and New Zealand.

Ingredients:

- 2 ounces Absolut Mandarin orange vodka
- ½ ounce banana liqueur
- 2 ounces pineapple juice
- 4 ounces ginger ale
- sugar (granulated)

Mixing Instructions:

Rim a Collins glass with granulated sugar. Combine the banana liqueur, Absolut Mandarin orange vodka, and pineapple juice in a cocktail shaker half-filled with ice. Shake well until blended and chilled. Strain into a Collins glass and top with the ginger ale. Garnish with an orange or pineapple wheel.

Moorea Blue Lagoon

Moorea is known as "The Island of Love," but the word Moorea actually means "yellow lizard" and is taken from the name of a family of Polynesian chiefs. The island of Moorea is shaped like a butterfly and contains two beautiful bays, Cook's Bay and Opunohu Bay. Perhaps the most striking features of Moorea are the jagged peaks and spires that give the island its unique profile. Mount Mouaroa is commonly referred to as "shark's tooth" because its shape is that of a shark's tooth and its image is used on the 100 French Pacific Franc (CFP) coin. Mount Tohiea has a small hole through the very top of the mountain, and Tahitian legend says that the hole was created when the ancient warrior Pai threw his spear through the mountain.

Ingredients:

- 1 ounce Ketel One vodka
- 1 ounce blue curaçao
- ½ ounce peach schnapps
- splash of fresh lime juice
- splash of fresh lemon juice
- lemon-lime soda (like Sprite or 7UP)

Mixing Instructions:

Combine all ingredients except the lemon-lime soda in a cocktail shaker half-filled with ice. Shake well until blended and chilled. Strain into a Collins glass or champagne flute. Top with the lemon-lime soda. Garnish as desired.

Bali Hai Martini

About Bali Hai

The famous *Bali Hai*, so alluringly sung about in the musical *South Pacific*, is usually likened to the island of Moorea. It wasn't until after he'd written *Tales of the South Pacific*, however, that James Michener actually visited Moorea. When he entered Moorea's Cook's Bay, surrounded by its dramatic mountain peaks, Michener said the scene was exactly what he had in mind when he "created" *Bali Hai*.

Ingredients:

- 1 ounce Absolut Citron vodka
- ½ ounce Cointreau
- ½ ounce DeKuyper Mad Melon (watermelon) liqueur
- 2 ounces grapefruit juice
- splash of fresh lime juice

Mixing Instructions:

Combine all ingredients in a cocktail shaker half-filled with ice. Shake well until blended and chilled. Strain into a Martini glass. Garnish as desired

Rangiroa, Water Sports Paradise

Rangiroa is the second-largest atoll in the world, stretching 42 miles long and 16 miles wide. As an atoll, Rangiroa exists as a narrow chain of white sand- and palm-strewn islands in the shape of a ring, with a large and very stunning turquoise lagoon in the center of the ring. Rangiroa's topography makes it an immense playground for water sports. Several ocean passes in the atoll allow sea life to enter and exit the interior lagoon with the changing tides, creating spectacular "drift" snorkeling and diving experiences.

Tahitian Cranilla Martini

Ingredients:

- 2 ounces Grey Goose la Vanille vodka
- 2 drops Tahitian vanilla extract
- ½ ounce simple syrup
- splash of cranberry juice
- splash of fresh lime juice

Mixing Instructions:

Combine all ingredients in a cocktail shaker half-filled with ice. Shake well until blended and chilled. Strain into a Martini glass. Garnish as desired.

Tropical Passion

Ingredients:

- 1 ounce Cruzan coconut rum
- ¾ ounce Chambord
- ½ ounce mango liqueur
- 4 ounces pineapple juice
- ½ ounce orange juice
- ½ ounce cranberry juice

Mixing Instructions:

Fill a hurricane glass half-full with ice. Add all ingredients. Stir to mix. Garnish as desired.

Archery, an Ancient Sport

In ancient Tahiti, archery was a sacred sport practiced only by people of high rank, such as Tahitian tribal princes. Archery platforms were located near stone temples and were off-limits, or *taboo*, to anyone else. Even though Tahitians were expert marksmen, they never used their bows and arrows as weapons of war. Today, remnants of the temples and archery platforms can be seen in the Opunohu Valley of Moorea and at the Fare Hape archeological site near the center of the island of Tahiti.

Mutiny on the Bounty

Moua Roa

The infamous British Captain Bligh sailed the HMS Bounty to Tahiti in 1788 on a mission to collect seedlings of breadfruit trees for planting in the West Indies. Legend has it that the crew loved Tahiti and its beautiful women so much they didn't want to return to the ordinary life of seamen, and instead desired to remain in paradise permanently. Shortly after leaving Tahiti, first mate Fletcher Christian led the famous mutiny on the Bounty and took control of the ship, returning it to Tahiti. Following the mutiny, Captain Bligh was cast adrift in a small open boat with 18 of his loyal men and successfully navigated for 41 days before arriving safely at Timor in Indonesia.

Ingredients:

- 2 ounces Grey Goose vodka
- ½ ounce Cruzan coconut rum
- 1½ ounces Midori melon liqueur
- ½ ounce banana liqueur
- ½ ounce half-and-half

Mixing Instructions:

Combine all ingredients in a cocktail shaker half-filled with ice. Shake well until blended and chilled. Strain into any chilled glass filled with ice. Garnish as desired.

Tahiti Martini

Ingredients:

- 1 ounce Ketel One vodka
- $\frac{1}{2}$ ounce blue curaçao
- $\frac{1}{2}$ ounce Bacardi Coco (coconut) rum
- $\frac{1}{4}$ ounce vanilla schnapps

Mixing Instructions:

Combine all ingredients in a cocktail shaker half-filled with ice. Shake well until blended and chilled. Strain into a Martini glass. Garnish with an orange twist.

Beautiful Black Pearls

Tahiti is one of the few places in the world where cultured black pearls are produced. The pearls form in marvelous colors, including silver gray, deep green iridescent with pink, gold, blue, and the darkest black. The infinite range of shades is natural and produced by the Pinctada Margaritifera, an oyster species common in Polynesia. The Tahiti Pearl Museum in Papeete highlights the black pearl's stature in ancient Tahitian art, history, mythology, and religion. Shops on nearly every island offer the pearls, but the best selections are found in Tahiti and Moorea.

Tamaaraa, Culinary Feast

On many of the islands, you can still experience the authentic Tahitian culinary feast called *tamaaraa*. Native Tahitian dishes of fish, roasted pork, and chicken are cooked in an underground oven pit called an *ahimaa*, which has been heated with volcanic stones. Polynesian dancing and singing accompany the feast.

Tahitian Rum Punch

Ingredients:

- 1 ½ ounces Bacardi light rum
- 1 ounce Mt. Gay Eclipse gold rum
- 1 ounce dry white wine
- 1 teaspoon crème de banana
- 1 ounce grapefruit juice
- 1 ounce orange juice
- 1 ounce pineapple juice
- ½ ounce fresh lime juice
- 1 teaspoon brown sugar
- 2 drops Tahitian vanilla extract

Mixing Instructions:

Dissolve the sugar in lime juice. Combine this mixture with the remaining ingredients in a cocktail shaker half-filled with ice. Shake well until blended and chilled. Strain into a highball or old-fashioned glass. Garnish with fruit and flowers.

Vanilla Mango Margarita

Flowering Jewelry

Tahitians love flowers and wear them like jewelry. Delicate flower necklaces called *leis* are used for greetings and are frequently worn around the neck and shoulders, while beautiful flower crowns called *heis* are worn on the head for special occasions. For daily wear, women often accentuate their hair with a bright hibiscus flower, and both men and women often place a tiaré flower behind one ear—on the left side if they're "taken," and on the right if they're "looking."

Ingredients:

- 2 ounces Jose Cuervo Especial gold tequila
- 1 ounce Grand Marnier
- 1 ounce Cruzan mango rum
- 1 ounce fresh lime juice
- 4 drops Tahitian vanilla extract
- sugar (granulated)

Mixing Instructions:

Rim a chilled margarita glass with granulated sugar. Combine the remaining ingredients in a blender with one cup ice. Blend well at high speed until smooth. Pour into a margarita glass. Garnish as desired.

Cocktails in Tahiti

Swaying Palm Tree

Ingredients:

- 1 ounce Midori melon liqueur
- 1 ounce Danzka vodka
- 1/2 ounce coconut liqueur
- 1/2 ounce Cointreau
- 1/2 ounce vanilla schnapps
- 3 ounces pineapple juice
- splash of fresh lime juice

Mixing Instructions:

Combine all ingredients in a cocktail shaker half-filled with ice. Shake well until blended and chilled. Strain into a Collins glass. Garnish as desired.

Tattoo, a Polynesian Custom

The word *tattoo* originated in Tahiti. The Tahitian legend of Tohu, the god of tattoo, describes the painting of all the oceans' fish in beautiful colors and patterns. This ancient Polynesian custom dates back hundreds of years and was often done without anesthetic. In Polynesian culture, tattoos have long been considered signs of beauty and in earlier times were ceremoniously applied when children reached adolescence. Many intricate Tahitian tattoo designs and symbols were developed and are still widely used today.

Copra, an Important Export

Copra, the sun-dried meat harvested from coconuts, is one of Tahiti's most important exports. The abundance of coconuts in the islands makes copra production extremely popular, and travelers to Tahiti will undoubtedly see open coconut shells being dried in the warm tropical sun. Once dried, the coconut meat is pressed to produce oil, which is used in many products and is a highly prized ingredient in soaps and lotions.

Coconut Dream

Ingredients:

- 1 ounce Captain Morgan spiced rum
- ¾ ounce white crème de cacao
- 1 ounce coconut cream
- 1½ ounces half-and-half

Mixing Instructions:

Combine all ingredients in a cocktail shaker half-filled with ice. Shake well until blended and chilled. Strain into a highball glass half-filled with ice cubes. Garnish as desired.

Mango Martini

Ancient Polynesian people were extremely spiritual and worshiped their gods in open-air sanctuaries known as *marae*. The ruins of many ancient marae can be seen throughout the islands of French Polynesia, with a very large concentration of ruins on the northeast side of Huahine. These massive stone temples had altars, platforms, and paved walkways. Entry into the marae by anyone other than the priests and the nobility was punishable by death.

Ingredients:

- 2 ounces Belvedere vodka
- 1/4 ounce lime juice
- 1 ounce triple sec
- 2 ounces mango juice

Mixing Instructions:

Combine all ingredients in a blender with one cup crushed ice. Blend well at high speed until smooth. Pour into a Martini glass. Garnish as desired.

Legends of Hiro

In Polynesian mythology, Hiro was a great Tahitian warrior and god of thieves. There are many legends about Hiro in Tahitian history, including the story of how Hiro used his great canoe to create a channel slicing the island of Huahine in half, forming Huahine Nui and Huahine Iti. It is said that Hiro's paddle and parts of his anatomy can be seen in the stone formations of the cliffs overlooking the channel.

Hiro's Sunsplash

Ingredients:

- 2½ ounces Skyy Orange vodka
- ½ ounce vanilla liqueur
- ½ ounce Chambord
- ½ ounce freshly squeezed lemon juice
- ½ ounce freshly squeezed orange juice
- ½ ounce cranberry juice

Mixing Instructions:

Combine all ingredients in a cocktail shaker half-filled with ice. Shake well until blended and chilled. Strain into any beverage glass filled with ice. Garnish with an orange wheel and cherry.

Taha'a Vanilla Martini

Most varieties of vanilla are naturally pollinated by birds or bees. Tahitian vanilla, however, must be pollinated by hand using a small wooden stick to insert the pollen into the plant. A fast worker can pollinate 2,000 plants each day. The plants must be pollinated the same day they bloom or the pods will not turn into vanilla beans. This process, called wedding, will cause the plants to "give birth" nine months later to vanilla pods about seven inches long. The vanilla pods will then be dried naturally in the warm Tahitian sun.

Ingredients:

- 1½ ounces Van Gogh pineapple vodka
- ¼ ounce vanilla schnapps
- ½ ounce crème de banana
- 2 drops Tahitian vanilla extract

Mixing Instructions:

Combine all ingredients in a cocktail shaker half-filled with ice. Shake well until blended and chilled. Strain into a Martini glass. Garnish as desired.

Breadfruit

The breadfruit, or Tahitian *uru*, is a grapefruit-sized fruit that grows abundantly throughout French Polynesia. The tree itself is quite large and has beautiful, waxy, interestingly shaped green leaves. The fruit is very rich in starch and, after cooking, tastes much like potato or baked bread. In addition to the food source, breadfruit tree bark is pounded into *tapa*, a form of highly prized cloth that was used by ancient Tahitians.

Caipirinha Tahiti

Ingredients:

- 2 ounces Cruzan light rum
- 1 small lime
- sugar to taste
- 2 drops Tahitian vanilla extract

Mixing Instructions:

Cut a small lime into pieces and place in a highball or old-fashioned glass. Add a sprinkle of sugar and muddle the ingredients to release the juice of the lime. Add the rum and vanilla, and fill the glass with crushed ice. Stir well. Garnish with lime wedges.

Tropical Lover

Mobile Restaurants

A common form of inexpensive "restaurant" in Tahiti is the *roulotte*. Named for their mobility, roulottes are well-appointed vans or trucks that are often parked along the waterfronts and serve a wide variety of good food. Each roulotte specializes in a particular type of food, such as seafood, pizza, Chinese, steak, and even crepes or ice cream. Many roulottes are found at the cruise ship dock in Papeete, where they're a hub for social activity on weekend evenings.

Ingredients:

- ¾ ounce Bacardi light rum
- ½ ounce Myers's dark rum
- ¾ ounce Stolichnaya vodka
- ¾ ounce Grand Marnier
- ½ ounce lemon juice
- 3 ounces mango juice

Mixing Instructions:

Combine all ingredients in a cocktail shaker half-filled with ice. Shake well until blended and chilled. Strain into a highball glass. Garnish as desired.

Cocktails in Tahiti

Midnight Rendezvous

Healing Properties

The *nono* or *noni* fruit grows abundantly in Tahiti and is said to have numerous healing properties. Polynesians historically used the noni fruit and its juice to soothe the sting of the poisonous stonefish and as a cure for sore throats. Today, several health food companies in Europe and North America are widely marketing noni juice as a nutritional supplement for improving digestive, respiratory, immune, and cardiac health.

Ingredients:

- 2 ounces Bombay Sapphire gin
- ½ ounce Bols parfait amour
- dash triple sec
- dash grenadine

Mixing Instructions:

Combine all ingredients in a cocktail shaker half-filled with ice. Shake well until blended and chilled. Strain into a Martini glass. Garnish as desired.

Ancient Fishing

The traditional Tahitian method of stone fishing is still performed during special festivals. Dozens of outrigger canoes form a semicircle off the beach, after which the men in the canoes beat the water with stones tied to ropes. The frightened fish are driven toward the beach while the men jump from the canoes yelling and beating the water with their hands to drive the fish ashore. The fish are then collected for the Tahitian feast called *tamaaraa*.

Zombie (Tahiti Style)

Ingredients:

- ½ ounce Myers's dark rum
- 1 ounce Bacardi light rum
- ½ ounce Demerara rum
- 1 ounce curaçao (white or blue)
- ¼ ounce grenadine
- ½ ounce simple syrup
- ½ ounce papaya juice or guava juice (optional)
- 1 ounce fresh lemon juice
- 1 ounce orange juice
- 1 ounce pineapple juice
- 3 drops Tahitian vanilla extract

Mixing Instructions:

Combine all ingredients in a blender with one cup ice. Blend well at high speed until smooth. Pour into a chilled Collins glass. Garnish as desired.

Torch Lighter

Ingredients:

- 1 ounce Cruzan coconut rum
- ¾ ounce Myers's dark rum
- ½ ounce banana liqueur
- 1 ounce passion fruit juice
- 1 ounce cranberry juice

Mixing Instructions:

In a highball glass, add the Cruzan coconut rum, followed by the banana liqueur, passion fruit juice, and cranberry juice. Stir, then top with Myers's dark rum. Garnish as desired.

Famous Resident: Gauguin

The famous French painter Paul Gauguin lived on the island of Tahiti in the 1890s and used Tahitian subjects in many of his lovely works. Known for his raucous behavior, Gauguin was forced to leave the island of Tahiti and moved to the island of Hiva Oa in the Marquesas, where he died and was buried. Today, Papeari, a town on the main island of Tahiti, is the site of the Paul Gauguin Museum. Most of Gauguin's paintings are privately owned, and one of the museum's most interesting displays is a detailed overview of the owners of each of his works.

Famous Resident: Brando

During the 1962 filming of *Mutiny on the Bounty* in Tahiti and Bora Bora, actor Marlon Brando fell in love with the islands and their stunning beauty. In 1965, Brando purchased the island of Tetiaroa, where he built a small resort and spent many years of his life. It is rumored that Brando, who died in 2004, granted his friend Michael Jackson lifelong use of a small motu off the west side of Tetiaroa. Today, a fantastic new eco-resort is being built on Tetiaroa.

Tetiaroa Delight

Ingredients:

- 1 ounce Ketel One vodka
- 1 1/2 ounces Cruzan light rum
- 6 strawberries
- 1 banana
- 1/2 ounce coconut milk
- 1/2 ounce lime juice
- 1/2 ounce grenadine
- 1 pinch ground cinnamon

Mixing Instructions:

Combine all ingredients except the cinnamon in a blender with one cup ice. Blend well at high speed until smooth. Pour into a Collins or hurricane glass and dust with the cinnamon. Garnish as desired.

Moana Passion

Ingredients:

- 2 ounces Bacardi light rum
- dash of crème de coconut liqueur
- 1/2 cup fresh mango
- 1/2 cup fresh papaya
- 2 ounces pineapple juice
- 1 ounce chopped macadamia nuts
- splash of half-and-half

Mixing Instructions:

Combine all ingredients in a blender with one cup ice. Blend well at high speed. Pour into a chilled Collins glass. Garnish as desired.

Tahiti's Favorite Sport

The closest thing to a national sport in Tahiti is pirogue (outrigger canoe) racing. The best time to see the races is during the Heiva festival in July. The biggest race of the year, however, is the Hawaiki Nui Va'a in mid-November. The Hawaiki Nui Va'a is the world's largest, longest, and most exhilarating international open-ocean outrigger canoe event. It's the ultimate test of strength and endurance, with six-person crews racing 72 miles from the islands of Huahine to Raiatea, then to Taha'a, and finally to Bora Bora. An entourage of avid fans follows the race in canoes and boats, creating a large and festive regatta.

Money Matters

Although Tahiti is an overseas territory of France, the Euro is not the currency used in Tahiti. Instead, Tahitians use the CFP, which is also used in the French dependency of New Caledonia, located between Tahiti and Australia. The CFP's paper currency varies in size according to the denomination and is bright and colorful, with landscapes and historical figures depicted on both sides.

Bora Bora Blue Cosmopolitan

Ingredients:

- 2 ounces Grey Goose le Citron vodka
- 1 ounce blue curaçao
- ½ ounce grapefruit juice
- ½ ounce simple syrup
- sugar (granulated)

Mixing Instructions:

Rim a chilled Martini glass with granulated sugar. Stir the remaining ingredients in a mixing glass with ice to prevent cloudiness. Strain into the Martini glass. If desired, garnish with a lemon twist.

MAI TAIS, THE LEGEND REVEALED

The Mai Tai is probably the most famous tropical cocktail of all. It's truly a classic whose original recipe has, unfortunately, been randomized and altered over the years. Today, few bartenders know how to make the original Mai Tai, and many adaptations of this delicious drink have evolved.

To pay proper respect to this Tahiti legend, it's important to understand the foundations of the recipe and to discover as much as possible about its history and origins. The Mai Tai was invented in Oakland, California, in 1944 by Victor "Trader Vic" Bergeron. It quickly became a popular drink throughout the world, but its original formula was a closely guarded secret. By 1970, however, Trader Vic had become so tired of others claiming to have invented the Mai Tai that he contacted the guests (who happened to be from Tahiti) for whom he first created the drink more than 25 years earlier. He had the guests sign an affidavit detailing how he had created an experimental cocktail for them, and, after tasting it, how they exclaimed "*Mai Tai—Roa Ae*," Tahitian for "Out of this world—the best." At this point, he also detailed his original recipe.

Today, a Mai Tai will often be served with pineapple juice, orange juice, and many other fruity additives in an attempt to increase its tropical flair. However, two fundamental ingredients that should be included are fresh lime juice and dark rum.

You can find the full story of Trader Vic's Mai Tai on his web site, www.TraderVics.com. Here's a brief excerpt:

by Victor J. "Trader Vic" Bergeron
San Francisco 1970

In 1944, after success with several exotic rum drinks, I felt a new drink was needed. I thought about all the really successful drinks; martinis, manhattans, daiquiris . . . . All basically simple drinks.

I was at the service bar in my Oakland restaurant. I took down a bottle of 17-year-old rum. It was J. Wray Nephew from Jamaica; surprisingly golden in color, medium bodied, but with the rich pungent flavor particular to the Jamaican blends. The flavor of this great rum wasn't meant to be overpowered with heavy additions of fruit juices and flavorings. I took a fresh lime, added some orange curacao from Holland, a dash of Rock Candy Syrup, and a dollop of French Orgeat, for its subtle almond flavor. A generous amount of shaved ice and vigorous shaking by hand produced the marriage I was after. Half the lime shell went in for color . . . I stuck in a branch of fresh mint and gave two of them to Ham and Carrie Guild, friends from Tahiti, who were there that night. Carrie took one sip and said, "Mai Tai - Roa Ae". In Tahitian this means "Out of This World - The Best". Well, that was that. I named the drink "Mai Tai".

The Original Mai Tai Formula, 1944

As originally created by Victor Bergeron

Ingredients:

- 2 ounces of 17-year-old J. Wray Nephew Jamaican rum
- ½ ounce French Garnier Orgeat Syrup
- ½ ounce Holland DeKuyper Orange Curaçao
- ¼ ounce Trader Vic's Rock Candy Syrup
- the juice from one fresh lime

Mixing Instructions:

Pour the 2 ounces of 17-year-old J. Wray & Nephew rum over shaved ice in a large glass. Add the lime juice. Add the Holland DeKuyper Orange Curaçao, Trader Vic's Rock Candy Syrup, and the French Ganrier Orgeat Syrup. Cover and shake vigorously by hand. Garnish with half of the lime shell inside the drink and float a sprig of fresh mint at the edge of the glass.

Mai Tai Bliss

Ingredients:

- 1 ounce Bacardi light rum
- 1 ounce Myers's dark rum
- ½ ounce triple sec
- ½ ounce amaretto
- 2 ounces fresh lime juice
- ½ ounce simple syrup

Mixing Instructions:

Combine all ingredients in a cocktail shaker half-filled with ice. Shake well until blended and chilled. Strain into a Collins or hurricane glass half-filled with ice.

Mai Tai Lagoon

Ingredients:

- 2 ounces Cruzan light rum
- 1 ounce blue curaçao
- ½ ounce amaretto
- ½ ounce grenadine
- ½ ounce fresh lime juice
- ½ teaspoon powdered sugar

Mixing Instructions:

Combine all ingredients in a cocktail shaker half-filled with ice. Shake well until blended and chilled. Strain into a Collins or hurricane glass half-filled with ice.

Mai Tai Dream

Ingredients:

- ½ ounce Captain Morgan spiced rum
- ½ ounce Bacardi light rum
- ½ ounce crème d'almond
- ½ ounce triple sec
- 2½ ounces orange juice
- 2½ ounces pineapple juice
- splash of lime juice

Mixing Instructions:

Combine all ingredients in a cocktail shaker half-filled with ice. Shake well until blended and chilled. Strain into a Collins or hurricane glass half-filled with ice.

Mai Tai Rangiroa

Ingredients

- ¾ ounce Myers's dark rum
- ¾ ounce Malibu coconut rum
- ¾ ounce Captain Morgan spiced rum
- ¾ ounce Grand Marnier
- juice of one lime
- splash of orange juice
- 2 ounces pineapple juice
- splash of vanilla extract
- splash of grenadine

Mixing Instructions:

Combine all of the ingredients except the Myers's dark rum in a cocktail shaker half-filled with ice. Shake well until blended and chilled. Strain into a Collins or hurricane glass half-filled with ice and float the Myers's dark rum on top.

MANIHI PEARL BEACH RESORT
Coconut's Pearl

Ingredients:

- 1⅓ ounces Bacardi light rum
- 1 ounce triple sec
- 1 scoop coconut ice cream
- 5 ounces fresh coconut water

Mixing Instructions:

Combine all ingredients in a blender. Blend well at high speed until smooth. Pour into a chilled hurricane glass or coconut shell. Garnish with grated coconut and tropical flowers.

Located on the atoll of Manihi in the Tuamotu Archipelago, the Manihi Pearl Beach Resort is beautifully integrated into its natural lagoon environment. With no other hotel on the island and just one small village nearby, you have the pristine beaches all to yourself, making this intimate resort a perfect yet comfortable getaway from civilization.

The Manihi Pearl Beach Resort is an example of tasteful, traditional Polynesian architecture, using a combination of precious local woods, bamboo, shells, and pandanus. The overwater bungalows have spacious sundecks suspended above the lagoon, providing guests with continuous views of the water's endless shades of blues and greens. The beach bungalows line a beautiful white sand beach and offer direct access to the lagoon.

The hotel's Poe Rava restaurant provides a dramatic view of the water and features many seafood dishes and continental favorites. The Miki Miki bar is nestled between a pure white sand beach, a lovely swimming pool, and the lagoon. A friendly, professional staff and some of Tahiti's best snorkeling among colorful coral gardens make this hotel a very special place.

HOTEL KIA ORA, RANGIROA

Secret Lagoon

Ingredients:

- 1 ounce vodka
- ½ ounce light rum
- ½ ounce triple sec
- ½ ounce fresh lemon juice
- ½ ounce simple syrup

Mixing Instructions:

Combine all ingredients in a blender with one cup ice. Blend well at high speed until smooth. Pour into a chilled margarita glass. Garnish as desired.

The Hotel Kia Ora is a delightful property in Rangiroa, one of the world's most spectacular diving locations. Located by a seemingly endless blue lagoon and gorgeous beach, this comfortable resort is ideal for water-sports enthusiasts and nature lovers.

The hotel offers garden, beach, and overwater bungalows all built completely in a Polynesian style, blending beautiful local materials with international-class comforts. The resort's beach bungalows feature private outdoor Jacuzzis.

At the charming overwater bar, guests can enjoy refreshing cocktails and magnificent sunsets. A beautiful open-air restaurant provides a relaxing atmosphere and exotic décor for guests to delight in the chef's original menu of tropical flavors, seafood specialties, and international dishes. A barbecue buffet Wednesday and Sunday evenings is accompanied by a Polynesian dance show and local music.

A wonderful excursion desk, beautiful pool, tennis courts, and excellent on-site diving company offer guests a full range of activities at this lovely resort.

TIKEHAU PEARL BEACH RESORT
Tikehau Pearl

Ingredients:

- 1 1/3 ounces vodka
- 2/3 ounce pear liqueur
- 2/3 ounce brandy
- 1/3 ounce triple sec
- 5 ounces guava juice

Mixing Instructions:

Combine all ingredients in a cocktail shaker half-filled with ice. Shake well until blended and chilled. Strain into a hurricane glass half-filled with ice cubes.

Located on the sparkling atoll of Tikehau, the Tikehau Pearl Beach Resort offers incredible scenery surrounded by one of nature's most perfect lagoons. Guests are met at the airport and transferred by speedboat directly to this lovely hotel, where they enjoy the exceptional blend of serenity, elegant informality, and Polynesian hospitality.

The hotel is located on a secluded white sand beach fringed with palm trees and offers well-appointed beach and overwater bungalows. The spacious Polynesian-style bungalows have private verandahs and are equipped with all the modern amenities.

The resort is surrounded by a string of uninhabited islands with pristine white and pink sand beaches. The islands are easily accessible from the hotel by a canoe or kayak, allowing guests to explore and spend their days in complete seclusion on any number of beautiful, undisturbed beaches.

The poolside bar and restaurant provide an ideal setting to observe the lagoon during the day and the shimmering stars at night. A variety of excursions are offered, including incredible diving and snorkeling in the pristine lagoon and visits to "Bird Island," home to hundreds of rare sea birds.

TE TIARÉ BEACH RESORT, HUAHINE
Passion Tiaré

Ingredients:

- 1¼ ounces vodka
- 1 ounce grenadine
- 1 ounce passion fruit juice
- 1 ounce orange juice

Mixing Instructions:

Combine all ingredients in a blender with one cup ice. Blend well at high speed until smooth. Pour into a hurricane glass. Garnish as desired.

Huahine's finest hotel, **the Te Tiaré Beach Resort,** is located on a private lagoon. Accessible only by boat from the village of Fare, guests visiting the resort will enjoy a lovely boat ride through the breathtaking turquoise lagoon.

Upon arrival at the resort, guests immediately discover just how different the Te Tiaré Beach Resort truly is. The hotel's lobby, lounge, main bar, restaurant, and boutiques are all built out over the lagoon in a design that is unique in French Polynesia.

The Te Tiaré's 41 spacious bungalows give the resort an intimate feeling and offer unsurpassed views of spectacular tropical sunsets, as well as views of the nearby islands of Raiatea and Taha'a.

Next to the lagoon, guests can enjoy the free-form swimming pool and beach bar as well as the resort's water sports center. Fine dining with spectacular ocean views is offered at the hotel's Ari'i restaurant serving French, Polynesian, and international cuisine.

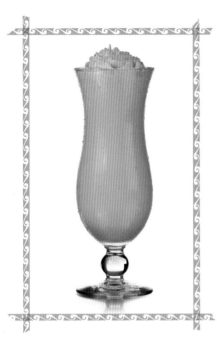

LE TAHA'A PRIVATE ISLAND & SPA

Le Taha'a Cocktail

Ingredients:

- 2 ounces light rum
- splash of Myers's dark rum
- 1 ounce coconut liqueur
- ½ ounce fresh coconut milk
- 1½ ounces banana juice
- 1½ bananas

Mixing Instructions:

Combine all ingredients in a blender and blend well at high speed until smooth. Pour into a hurricane glass half-filled with ice. Garnish as desired.

Le Taha'a Private Island & Spa is a lavish resort designed to deliver the ultimate in luxury and service, starting with guests' private speedboat transfer from the airport. A Relais & Chateaux member, Le Taha'a is superbly located on Motu Tautau, facing Taha'a island and offering an unsurpassed view of Bora Bora.

The overwater suites and beach villas, considered by many to be the best in Tahiti, are beautifully styled and feature spacious lounges, terraces, private decks, and world-class amenities. The overwater suites offer direct access to the lagoon, and beach villas feature private gardens with plunge pools.

The elegantly designed public areas are elevated, providing exquisite tree-top views of the lagoon and Taha'a island. A poolside grill, open-air dining room, and special gourmet restaurant feature superb cuisine combining the best in local ingredients with traditional favorites.

The resort offers tennis courts, an elegant swimming pool, dive center, and a wide range of excursions, while the splendid Manea Spa pampers guests with the finest in Tahitian treatments and therapies.

HOTEL BORA BORA

Poerava (means "Tahitian Black Pearl")

Ingredients:

- 1 ounce amaretto almond liqueur
- ⅔ ounce Midori melon liqueur
- ⅔ ounce blue curaçao
- 1 ounce Bailey's Irish Cream
- 5 ounces banana juice

Mixing Instructions:

Combine all ingredients in a cocktail shaker half-filled with ice. Shake well until blended and chilled. Strain into a Collins glass half-filled with ice cubes. Garnish as desired.

Sitting beside a turquoise lagoon beneath the lush, green volcanic peaks of Mount Otemanu, the **Hotel Bora Bora** is the quintessential symbol of French Polynesia and is consistently rated one of the world's top hotels. Like its island, the hotel nears exquisite perfection in its idyllic setting on Point Raititi, as guests see for themselves in a private boat trip from the airport.

The hotel is surrounded by immaculate, mature gardens with over 100 varieties of trees and plants. Three sugar-white beaches flank a lagoon in which every color of the rainbow shimmers among the sea life. Spacious villas and bungalows in a variety of settings are adorned with the finest classic furnishings.

The sun sets directly in front of the hotel, off the main beach, and some of the island's best snorkeling can be found in its lagoon. The Matira bar offers a warm and inviting atmosphere for relaxing, while the Matira Terrace restaurant features an outstanding menu and is widely considered the best restaurant in Bora Bora. Service is exceptional and understated elegance is the rule at this fantastic, intimate resort.

BORA BORA PEARL BEACH RESORT & SPA

Te Moana

Ingredients:

- 1½ ounces light rum
- 2½ ounces pineapple juice
- 2½ ounces coconut milk
- ⅔ ounce blue curaçao

Mixing Instructions:

Combine white rum, coconut milk, and pineapple juice in a cocktail shaker half-filled with ice. Shake well until blended and chilled. Strain into a hurricane glass half-filled with ice cubes. Top with blue curaçao. Garnish with fruit and tropical flowers.

The splendid **Bora Bora Pearl Beach Resort** is located on the private motu Tevairoa and offers dazzling views of majestic Mount Otemanu. Guests are met at the airport by speedboat and transferred directly to the hotel. One of the "Leading Small Hotels of the World," this beautiful resort features overwater bungalows, beach bungalow suites, and garden pool suites. Accommodations are splendidly appointed with fine local woods, tapa fabrics, and all of the amenities of a sophisticated luxury resort. Each bungalow and suite has a spacious bedroom, bathroom, and sun terrace.

The hotel's main restaurant, Tevairoa, is elevated to provide dramatic views of the lagoon and Mount Otemanu. The restaurant offers refined international cuisine and features special Polynesian shows for guests to enjoy while dining under the stars on the terrace.

The Bora Bora Pearl Beach Resort features a large swimming pool at the base of a waterfall. The hotel's new full-service Manea Spa is the largest spa in Tahiti and features special local products to enhance guests' spa experience. The resort also offers two boutiques, movie theater, poolside grill, bar, and an excellent diving center.

BORA BORA NUI RESORT & SPA

Bora Bora Nui Cocktail

Ingredients:

- 2 ounces dark rum
- ⅔ ounce Napoleon Mandarine liqueur
- ⅓ ounce banana liqueur
- ⅓ ounce Midori melon liqueur

- 1⅓ ounces papaya juice
- 1⅓ ounces passion fruit juice
- 1 teaspoon strawberry jam
- 1⅓ ounces coconut milk
- 1 Tahitian vanilla bean

Mixing Instructions:

Combine all ingredients, except the vanilla bean, in a blender with one cup ice. Blend well at high speed until smooth. Pour into a chilled hurricane glass or coconut shell. Garnish with the vanilla bean or as desired.

Located on the private island of Motu Toopua, in Bora Bora's magnificent blue lagoon, the incredible **Bora Bora Nui Resort & Spa** is situated on 16 acres of lush, terraced hillside surrounding a protected azure cove. Guests are met at the airport by speedboat and transferred directly to the hotel. One of the most luxurious resorts in the South Pacific, the Bora Bora Nui sets a benchmark for elegance and service. The resort's overwater check-in area sits atop a natural aquarium, while Bora Bora's largest white sand beach completes the setting.

The hotel offers overwater, beach, and hillside villas and lagoon-view suites. Built in fine Tahitian style, accommodations range in size from 1,000 to 1,500 square feet and are luxuriously appointed with rich, natural woods. All villas feature living rooms, bedrooms, large marble bathrooms, expansive shaded terraces, and sun decks.

Guests enjoy the large infinity swimming pool, three fine restaurants, and the excellent Mandara Spa, offering an extensive menu of unique treatments and services, making the Bora Bora Nui Resort the ultimate luxury hideaway.

BORA BORA INTERCONTINENTAL RESORT AND THALASSO SPA

Give Me a Kiss*

Ingredients:

- 2 ounces light rum
- 1 ounce raspberry liqueur
- 1/2 ounce banana juice
- 1/2 ounce lemon juice

Mixing Instructions:

Combine all ingredients in a blender with one cup ice. Blend well at high speed until smooth. Pour into a chilled cocktail glass. Garnish as desired.

From Sebastien Pires, Chief Barman at the InterContinental Resort

Situated on a motu along the legendary northeast side of Bora Bora, the dazzling **InterContinental Resort and Thalasso Spa** features 80 overwater villas surrounded by a beautiful turquoise lagoon and stunning views. This deluxe resort is unique beyond compare, where modern architecture and technology flourish side by side with traditional local arts and crafts. Guests are transferred by speedboat from the airport to the resort, where they experience the first Thalasso and Balneo spa center in the Southern Hemisphere.

This outstanding property offers some of the most luxurious accommodations in the Pacific. Each 1,000-square-foot overwater villa is designed with authentic Polynesian materials for an elegant, understated, but distinctly South Pacific décor. Villas have a spacious living room, bedroom with walk-in dressing room, opulent bathroom, and two flat-screen televisions with DVD players. In addition, each villa features a large shaded terrace with lounge chairs and dining table, as well as a spacious sun deck overlooking the lagoon.

Guests enjoy a lovely white sand beach stretching over 1,000 feet, a magnificent infinity pool, two restaurants and bars, conference facilities, and tennis courts.

Cocktails in Tahiti

ST. REGIS RESORT, BORA BORA

Mahana Magic

Ingredients:

- 1 ounce Belvedere vodka
- 1 ounce DeKuyper Island Blue Schnapps
- 1/4 ounce fresh lime juice
- splash of soda water

Mixing Instructions:

Combine all ingredients (except the soda water) in a cocktail shaker half-filled with ice. Shake well until blended and chilled. Strain into an old-fashioned glass. Top with soda water. Garnish as desired.

The St. Regis Resort, Bora Bora, is the epitome of elegance and paradise. Edged by powdery sands and a tranquil lagoon, the resort is situated below the towering majesty of Mount Otemanu, an ever-present symbol of the lofty luxury and impressively personalized service of this exceptional hotel.

Following a pleasant private-boat trip from the airport, guests are escorted to one of the resort's gorgeous villas magnificently appointed to ensure the ultimate in comfort. There are 74 one-bedroom villas stretching over the lagoon; several feature terrace Jacuzzis. The five two-bedroom overwater villas with private swimming pools are a first in French Polynesia. Exquisite beach villas are also available.

Guests are delighted with the hotel's three restaurants. In addition, the resort offers a main pool with swim-up bar and a romantic adult pool with private daybeds. The spa—on its own private lagoon island—offers a state-of-the-art fitness center and an incomparable array of island-inspired indulgences.

The celebrated St. Regis Butler ensures that everything is possible for the hotel's guests. In every way, St. Regis Resort, Bora Bora, is the ultimate resort experience.

SOFITEL MOTU, BORA BORA

Otime

Ingredients:

- 1 ounce tequila
- ½ ounce coconut liqueur
- ½ ounce green crème de menthe
- 3½ ounces pineapple juice

Mixing Instructions:

Combine all ingredients in a blender with one cup ice. Blend well at high speed until smooth. Pour into a chilled beverage glass. Garnish as desired.

Located on a private island in Bora Bora's stunning lagoon, the Sofitel Motu is one of the island's most intimate resorts and a haven of peaceful, natural beauty.

Blending perfectly with its environment, the resort fully capitalizes on its stunning setting—as guests discover the second they see the hotel during their speedboat transfer from the airport. The 30 land and overwater bungalows offer breathtaking views of Bora Bora and its famous lagoon. Each is tastefully designed and decorated with native materials and the best modern comforts.

The lovely, secluded island features a bird sanctuary, short nature trails, three private cove beaches, and expansive coral gardens offering incredible snorkeling opportunities. To carefully preserve its quiet exclusivity, the island is restricted solely to registered hotel guests. The hotel's restaurant and lounge serve exceptional, award-winning cuisine. In addition to the lush charms of the Sofitel Motu, guests may also enjoy the amenities of its sister property, the nearby Sofitel Marara.

The Sofitel Motu's small, intimate size and serene atmosphere make it the perfect place for a quiet, relaxing, memorable vacation.

INTERCONTINENTAL LE MOANA RESORT, BORA BORA

Cocktail Bora Bora

Ingredients:

- ⅔ ounce light rum
- ⅔ ounce dark rum
- ⅓ ounce crème de cacao
- 1 scoop coconut ice cream
- 4 ounces pineapple juice

Mixing Instructions:

In a blender, combine the coconut ice cream and pineapple juice. Blend until creamy. Add the remaining ingredients and blend until mixed. Pour into a Collins glass. Garnish as desired.

An intimate hotel adorned by white sand beaches and turquoise water, Bora Bora's InterContinental Le Moana Resort delivers an exclusive, exotic retreat for an unforgettable vacation. The hotel's beach and overwater bungalows are jewels of traditional Tahitian architecture, designed in the purest Polynesian style and enhanced by the finest materials.

All bungalows are junior-size suites with a large sun terrace, living room, bedroom, and private bath. The unique Tahitian decor includes free-growing vanilla vines draping the bathroom walls and ceilings.

Guests begin their visit with a speedboat transfer from the airport and, upon arrival, discover a lovely, two-tiered pool surrounded by beautiful flower gardens. The resort is located on spectacular Matira Point, providing convenient access to shopping and the village, as well as excellent snorkeling among the nearby coral heads in the lagoon. The exceptional Noa Noa restaurant and beautiful bar offer nightly entertainment and make the Le Moana a wonderful "destination" resort.

LE MERIDIEN, BORA BORA

Sweet Vahine Mudslide

Ingredients:

- 1⅓ ounces Bailey's Irish Cream
- ⅓ ounce crème de cacao
- ⅓ ounce Kahlua coffee liqueur
- 2 ounces coconut milk

Mixing Instructions:

Combine all ingredients in a cocktail shaker half-filled with ice. Shake well until blended and chilled. Strain into an old-fashioned or highball glass half-filled with ice cubes. Garnish with a tropical flower.

Le Meridien is one of Bora Bora's finest resorts. Situated on the southern tip of a large motu, the resort has incredible views of Bora Bora and Raiatea. Following a refreshing speedboat transfer from the airport, guests discover 82 overwater bungalows and 18 beach bungalows that feature sumptuous architecture and sophisticated décor blending French flair and Tahitian style. All bungalows include a large bedroom with living area, spacious bathroom, and outdoor terrace. The ultimate touch in the overwater bungalows is a large glass panel in the living room floor for admiring marine life in the lagoon below.

The resort is surrounded by some of Bora Bora's best white sand beaches and a clear azure lagoon. Le Meridien offers several restaurants, bars, and a wide range of activities, including spa services. A unique feature is a turtle care sanctuary, where the resort participates in the protection and rehabilitation of endangered native sea turtles, as well as their successful release back into the ocean. Hotel guests are invited to participate in the activities of the turtle sanctuary.

SHERATON MOOREA LAGOON RESORT & SPA

Royal Tahiti

Ingredients:

- 1⅓ ounces dark rum
- 2 ounces banana juice
- ⅓ ounce strawberry syrup
- ⅔ ounce fresh lemon juice
- 2 scoops coconut ice cream

Mixing Instructions:

Combine all ingredients in a blender. Blend well at high speed until smooth. Pour into a chilled hurricane glass. Garnish as desired.

The Sheraton Moorea Lagoon Resort and Spa offers a beautiful, relaxing environment where guests have front-row seats to magnificent sunrises and sunsets. The beautifully landscaped property is located on one of Moorea's most stunning sites, offering exceptional views of Opunohu and Cook's Bays.

Spanning a lovely white sand beach along the shores of a crystal blue lagoon, the resort features gorgeous garden, beach, and overwater bungalows. Each is equipped with all the modern conveniences found in a world-class hotel, including special touches like claw-footed tubs.

From casual fare to extraordinary gourmet creations, visitors are certain to enjoy the hotel's restaurants. The resort's overwater bar is a popular gathering place to enjoy a cocktail while gazing at a tropical sunset or starlit sky. Nightly entertainment is offered throughout the property, and the concierge will be happy to arrange any number of activities. Guests will certainly want to take advantage of the fitness center, stunning infinity pool, and tennis courts, as well as the hotel's Mandara Spa, where numerous wraps, massages, and other treatments ensure that each guest's visit is relaxing and memorable.

MOOREA PEARL BEACH RESORT & SPA

Royal Moorea

Ingredients:

- ½ ounce Grand Marnier
- ½ ounce pineapple liqueur
- ½ ounce peach liqueur

- dash of simple syrup
- dash of fresh lime juice
- 1 ounce champagne

Mixing Instructions:

Combine all ingredients except champagne in a cocktail shaker half-filled with ice. Shake well until blended and chilled. Strain into a hurricane glass, wine glass, or champagne flute half-filled with ice cubes. Top with the champagne.

The fantastic **Moorea Pearl Beach Resort** is situated on 21 acres of gardens and white sand beachfront. Just two miles from enchanting Cook's Bay, the hotel is located conveniently near several small shops and restaurants. This traditional Polynesian style hotel offers garden rooms, garden bungalows, beach bungalows, and overwater bungalows. All bungalows have a large sundeck and sitting area. The overwater bungalows have direct access to the water and glass tables for watching the fascinating sea life below. Deluxe garden bungalows feature a small courtyard with private plunge pool.

The hotel features a beautiful infinity swimming pool and offers a wide range of activities and excursions, including an on-site dive center. The resort's Mandara Spa provides an excellent variety of services and treatments specializing in the use of locally grown products. The attractive open-air restaurant and large cocktail bar overlook the pool, beach, and lagoon and create a lovely setting for drinks or dining. The hotel also features a smaller gourmet restaurant with wonderful service and an outstanding, distinctive cuisine.

INTERCONTINENTAL RESORT & SPA, MOOREA

Cocoa Banana

Ingredients:

- 2 ounces light rum
- ⅔ ounce coconut liqueur
- 1 ounce crème de cacao
- 3½ ounces banana juice
- 2 scoops coconut ice cream

Mixing Instructions:

Combine all ingredients in a blender. Blend well at high speed until smooth. Pour into a chilled hurricane glass. Garnish as desired.

Close to Opunohu Bay on Moorea's northeast coast, the InterContinental Resort & Spa is a spectacular complex. Situated between dramatic mountains and Moorea's sparkling lagoon, the hotel provides all the comforts of a refined international resort. The property encompasses 27 acres of magnificent gardens with more than 165 species of trees, plants, and flowers.

The resort features garden, beach, and overwater bungalows, as well as garden lanai rooms. The bungalows are suites with a bedroom, separate sitting room, private bath, and spacious terrace, and all accommodations are designed in an elegant Polynesian style.

At the Fare Nui Restaurant, gourmet surprises and breathtaking ocean views ensure a memorable dining experience. The Fare Hana Restaurant serves simple, fresh food in a casual poolside setting.

The full-service Helene Spa provides treatments and massage therapies based on exotic native plants, flowers, and fruits. The Dolphin Quest Adventure Program, led by marine mammal experts, offers interactive experiences with these amazing and intelligent creatures. The hotel also features tennis courts, large swimming pool, beautiful cocktail bar, and nightly entertainment.

INTERCONTINENTAL RESORT, TAHITI

*Toe to Toe**

Ingredients:

- 2 ounces light rum
- 1 ounce green crème de menthe
- ½ ounce orange juice
- ½ ounce watermelon juice

Mixing Instructions:

Combine all ingredients in a blender. Blend well at high speed until smooth. Pour into a chilled high ball glass filled with ice. Garnish as desired.

From Sebastien Pires, Chief Barman at the InterContinental Resort

The Tahiti InterContinental Resort is a premier international hotel encompassing 30 lush tropical acres around a multi-colored lagoon and commanding a spectacular view of the island of Moorea. This lovely resort offers ocean- and garden-view rooms, as well as overwater bungalows. All accommodations are decorated in a tasteful and relaxing colonial Polynesian theme and offer private balconies.

The Tahiti InterContinental takes great pride in its excellent restaurants. The Tiaré restaurant serves exquisitely prepared French and international cuisine and Polynesian specialties, and offers theme nights featuring the country's best Tahitian dance show, Les Grands Ballets de Tahiti. The hotel's famous Le Lotus restaurant is beautifully situated over the lagoon and offers elegant gourmet dining in a refined and romantic atmosphere.

Guests can relax in two lovely infinity pools or enjoy snorkeling in the hotel's dynamic interactive lagoonarium. An aquatic center, tennis courts, and full-service activities desk provide guests numerous options for enjoying this charming resort.

LE MERIDIEN, TAHITI

Vanilla Fenua

Ingredients:

- ⅔ ounce dark rum
- ⅔ ounce amaretto
- 3½ ounces mango juice
- 1 ounce champagne
- 1 Tahitian vanilla bean

Mixing Instructions:

Combine dark rum and amaretto in a cocktail shaker half-filled with ice. Grate a small portion of the vanilla bean into the cocktail shaker. Shake well until blended and chilled. Strain into a Collins glass or Champagne flute. Add the mango juice and top with Champagne. If desired, garnish with the rest of the vanilla bean.

Le Meridien, Tahiti, is a lovely beachfront resort commanding beautiful views across the Sea of Moons to the island of Moorea. The resort offers deluxe rooms and overwater bungalows. All accommodations feature exceptional views of the ocean and a décor blending harmoniously with the hotel's Polynesian-style interior, with an emphasis on natural materials and local colors. In the superb overwater bungalows, guests enjoy every comfort, including a spacious living area opening onto an outdoor deck with direct lagoon access.

The hotel's signature feature is the spectacular beachfront sand-bottom swimming pool designed with beautiful coves. The hotel also offers tennis courts and a variety of excursions and activities.

There is a charming pool bar in addition to a larger open-air bar. La Plantation restaurant offers international, Polynesian, and seafood dishes and features fabulous Tahitian dance shows several times each week. Le Carré is the hotel's special gourmet restaurant, offering upscale dining with exceptional, panoramic views of Moorea.

SHERATON HOTEL, TAHITI

Royal Maeva

Ingredients:

- 1 ounce light rum
- ½ ounce Bols raspberry (framboise) liqueur
- ½ ounce coconut liqueur
- dash of fresh lime juice
- sugar (granulated)

Mixing Instructions:

Rim a highball or old-fashioned glass with sugar and fill with ice cubes. Combine the remaining ingredients in a cocktail shaker half-filled with ice. Shake well until blended and chilled. Strain into the glass. Garnish as desired.

Sheraton Hotel, Tahiti, offers 200 guest rooms and suites, each decorated with authentic native materials. All accommodations feature panoramic views of a turquoise lagoon, Papeete Harbor, and the island of Moorea rising dramatically in the distance.

From innovative preparations of fresh seafood to casual alfresco dining under the stars, guests enjoy the hotel's unique overwater restaurant, sunset bar, and lounge.

The property is fully equipped with state-of-the-art facilities for business travelers and meeting attendees, yet offers all of the necessities of a carefree, fun vacation, including an infinity pool, Jacuzzi, and nightly entertainment.

The hotel's Mandara Spa embraces the healing traditions of the islands to create treatments using local ingredients like coconut milk, ginger, tiaré flowers, and aromatic vanilla beans.

With its convenient location and traditional resort amenities, the Sheraton Hotel, Tahiti, is a comfortable base for exploring Papeete and the main island of Tahiti.

Index